P9-BJE-707

WOMEN'S BODYBUILDING
PHOTO BOOK

WOMEN'S BODYBUILDING PHOTO BOOK

BY THE EDITORS OF *FIT* MAGAZINE

ANDERSON WORLD
BOOKS, INC.

©1983 by
Anderson World Books, Inc.

No information in this book may be reproduced
without permission from the publisher.

Anderson World Books, Inc.
1400 Stierlin Road
Mountain View, CA 94043

Robert Mapplethorpe photographs of Lisa Lyon are published
with the permission of Viking Press, Inc. ©1983, publishers of *Lady*.

Book design by Kevin J. Moran.

ISBN 0-89037-267-5

CONTENTS

INTRODUCTION: THE BLOSSOMING OF A NATIONAL MANIA

by Lou Ferrigno

A wonderful revolution has occurred in America. People are taking charge of their lives and doing something positive about their own fitness and health. In typical American fashion, if someone had tried to force fitness and health upon us, we'd have rebelled. But also in typical American fashion, once we get an idea, nothing in the world can stop us from pursuing it.

It is encouraging to see so many people exercising and becoming more conscious of the food they eat. I've been traveling quite a bit lately, doing feature films in Europe, and when I'm over there, I am always struck by the contrast with the United States. But I've noticed a genuine curiosity by Europeans about what their American friends are up to. "What's all this thing about fitness over in the United States?" they would ask me a few years ago, aware that I've long been a proponent of fitness and health and body development, and expecting that I'd have all the answers.

"I don't know, exactly," I'd tell them. "People seem to have suddenly realized what the experts have been trying to tell them all along: Only you can take control of your body and what happens to it." By now, though, Europeans are used to our fitness explosion, and some of our enthusiasm has rubbed off on them. I see more and more European people bicycling and walking and running than ever before.

Today, their questions are more precise. They want to know about the types of fitness Americans practice. One of their strongest interests is in women's bodybuilding, which I predict Europeans will take up with a passion once it catches on.

What I can tell them is that in America, interest in bodybuilding and strength training among women has blossomed. I can still remember the shock waves sent through the male-dominated world of bodybuilding in the late 1970s when women started working out in gyms. The ladies took some razzing at first, but once the male bodybuilders saw that they were serious about the sport, they accepted their female counterparts.

Women's bodybuilding has been blessed with some dedicated pioneers in the sport, who have made the rapid growth of bodybuilding possible. Without the persistence of those first women, the sport never would have become so popular. I'd like to salute those trailblazers' fortitude and dedication. They broke hallowed ground and planted some flowers that have blossomed beautifully. They've been a real asset to the sport, and I'm happy to see that they are now beginning to be noticed and appreciated.

I'm very pleased to have this opportunity to acknowledge my female colleagues in this most exciting of body-oriented sports. My wife and I believe strongly in being healthy, and the revolution in strength training and bodybuilding for women can only make women stronger and healthier. Be strong, be fit, be happy.

PART ONE: WOMEN BODYBUILDERS

LISA LYON

Lisa Lyon took up bodybuilding when it was hardly the thing for a young woman to do. But Lyon was undaunted. "I don't need anybody to tell me that what I do is OK," she said in an interview with *Fit* magazine. "What I do I did before I ever did any articles, and I'd be doing it if nobody knew who I was. I didn't care. I did it because I liked doing it."

The trailblazer for other women, Lyon went about sculpting her body into a shape that was both strong and aesthetically pleasing. Even after she had built up her muscles, she never lost her feminine silhouette or her soft, sleek appearance. Such a blend of strength and beauty was what the judges liked: Lyon won the first World Women's Bodybuilding Championship in 1979.

Since then, Lyon has ventured into other areas and out of competitive bodybuilding. Most recently, she completed work on a photographic book entitled *Lady.* Whatever direction Lyon's career may take her, she will always be remembered as the first lady of bodybuilding.

10

13

14

17

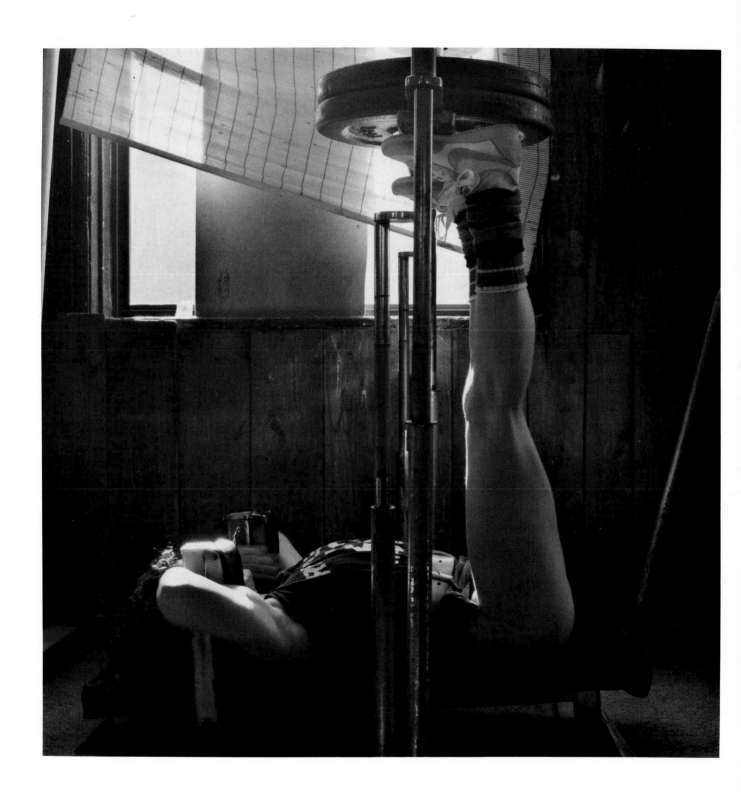

18

19

20

21

MICHELLE HOWE

Michelle Howe of Riverside, California, has been a bodybuilder for only a year and a half, but she has committed herself to the discipline whole-heartedly, and has every intention of being the best she can be.

Strange as it may seem, Howe got into bodybuilding as a result of an injury to her knee. She had surgery and then paid regular visits to a physical therapist to get the knee back in shape. Her orthopedic surgeon suggested she start lifting weights to rebuild the muscles.

Howe, who is a mere 20 years of age, wants to compete for a few years yet, and test herself against better bodybuilders. Part of what has given her the drive to improve and challenge herself, she believes, is her constant exposure to male bodybuilders, who have pushed her every step of the way. She has always worked out with men, which has been all to her advantage. As a result, she says, "I don't feel like a sissy." She currently works at the Spectrum Health and Fitness Center in Riverside.

24

25

30

JUDY HAYES

While some women dabble in bodybuilding or other sports for their own enjoyment and fitness without considering competition, Judy Hayes-Ferguson knew from the very beginning that she would be a competitor. "For me," she says, "competition was inevitable from the first time I could see my own muscles." Ferguson took up bodybuilding after her husband bought her a set of weights. She started playing around with them and once she saw the results, she decided to get serious about it. After only a year of working out, she entered her first contest, in 1983, the Miss Santa Cruz Classic in Santa Cruz, California, and won.

Ferguson balances her weight training with aerobic workouts, running about 20 to 25 miles a week and riding her bike another 40 miles. She sets goals for herself to keep motivated, but they must be goals that are attainable and reasonable. Right now, Ferguson's goal is just to keep competing and be the best bodybuilder she can be.

34

37

39

40

41

43

CHERYL HOWARD

For those of you skeptics who still think that muscles on a woman's body are unattractive, Cheryl Howard, if she can't convince you with her body, might convince you with her belief about what bodybuilding can do for a woman. "It enhances femininity," she says, "especially if you carry yourself the right way. The idea is not to be the best imitation of a man, but to bring out the best in a woman's body. That's the goal. Because a toned, fit body is more feminine."

For someone who's been competitive in bodybuilding for just one year, 29-year-old Howard has a pretty sound argument for why she does what she does. In 1982, she won the Golden Valley Physique Classic in Burbank, California, and in 1983, she capped third place in the Southern California Bodybuilding competition.

When she's not working out, Howard, who lives in Santa Monica, California, teaches physical education to retarded children. She plans on returning to school to earn another credential to allow her to teach general subjects in the classroom.

48

50

52

53

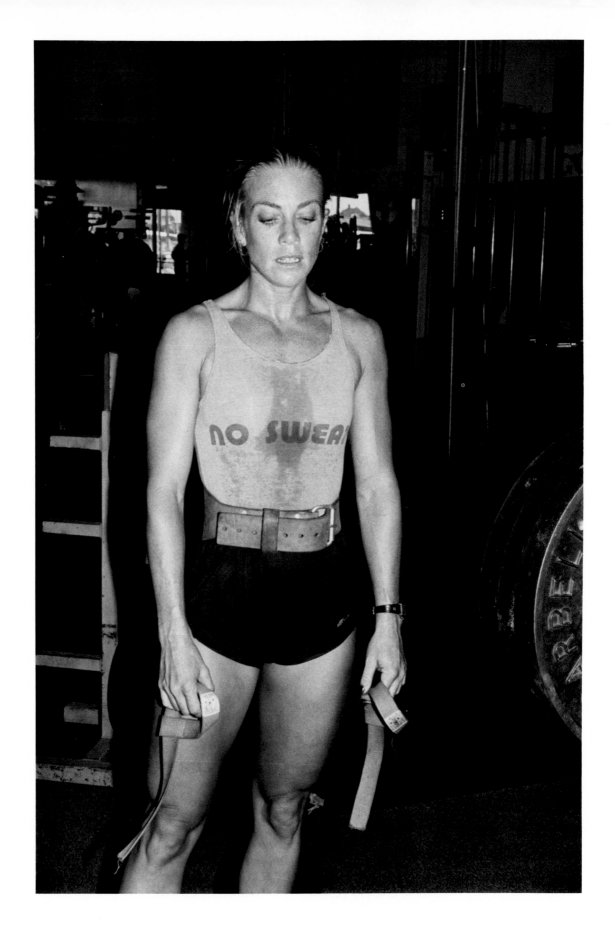

54

55

57

REGGIE BENNETT

She looks maybe 28 and sounds and acts at least that age. And she's got the down-to-earth attitude of a worldly-wise woman who's done her share of living. Believe she's a mere 22 years old? It's true. And if Reggie Bennett has anything to say about it, she'll be in the public eye for a long time to come. In the next two years, she hopes to be crowned Ms. Olympia, the highest honor a female bodybuilder can receive.

Bennett moved to Venice, California a year ago from San Antonio, Texas, where she had lived since age 17. Since then, she has had pretty good luck, having landed roles in the movies *"Spacehunter"* and *"The Man Who Loved Women."* Between film work and bodybuilding competitions, Bennett trains individual clients in bodybuilding. And when she's not working, she's usually working out. She trains year-round, starting her day with a 1½-hour aerobics class and a run. She then rides her bike to the gym to train a few people and spends 45 minutes to an hour working out. Then she goes for another run.

65

69

PATSY CHAPMAN

In 1979, women's bodybuilding made a major leap forward. Suddenly the sport was able to stand on its own two feet instead of merely being an adjunct to the men's competition. That same year, Patsy Chapman, a journalist from Michigan, won the title of Best in the World, the contest that evolved into Ms. Olympia extravaganza.

"For women, it all started in 1979," Chapman said recently. "It was the year when we were recognized as a force to be dealt with."

Chapman's professional career took a turn then. She had been a journalist since college, but had always harbored a desire to be a policewoman. She responded to an advertisement by the city of Houston for young, healthy men and women police officers and moved to Houston to train in police sciences. Her interest in bodybuilding took a back seat—at least until she was on the street in her uniform. She currently works the night shift and is able to put in a two-hour workout at the gym before coming to work.

72

74

75

80

CHRIS GLASS

"I'll be there, you watch." The warning is from Chris Glass, a determined young woman gearing up to re-enter competitive women's bodybuilding. Glass took a year off to have her baby, and now, 70 pounds lighter and just as determined, she is maintaining her muscle tone and keeping aerobically fit for a full-fledged training program.

Scheduling a workout into her already full day is no easy task for Glass. When she works out, she must wait until after dinner and the baby is asleep to bike to the gym. Some days she just can't make it, so she compromises with a long walk 1981, she was crowned Miss Indio, Miss Mission Viejo and Miss Los Angeles. An individual sport requiring a lot of self-motivation, bodybuilding takes energy and a strong mental attitude. "You can't be lazy about it," Glass says. Laziness is one trait Glass will never be accused of.

84

86

89

92

93

MICHELLE TIERNEY

If strength comes from discipline and discipline comes from commitment, Michele Tierney of San Diego is more than halfway to success in the competitive field of women's bodybuilding. With a background in human physiology, Tierney is one of the most knowledgeable of her peers on the functions of the body. Tierney has worked at a variety of jobs, from legal secretary to a bunny at a Playboy Club. She sees each new job as an opportunity to broaden her experiences and develop new friends.

Tierney has written about women's bodybuilding for such magazines as *Fit,* and has done some modeling for *Strength Training for Beauty,* a magazine on women's weight training and bodybuilding. She is outspoken against the use of anabolic steroids to add bulk and definition. "I think the tendency of some judges to want women bodybuilders to conform to objectives governing men's bodybuilding is going to be short-lived and fortunately will be countered by a group of judges who understand that you can be both developed and feminine at the same time," she says.

98

99

101

102

104

105

PART TWO: PUTTING IT TO THE TEST

THE COMPETITION

Every life needs a goal. And in life, there are goals within goals. For bodybuilders, the ultimate goal is to be the most perfectly developed physical specimen that their bodies, minds, discipline and commitment will allow. To succeed, however, they must set short-term goals along the way. And the most important are competitions.

Bodybuilding competitions–strenuous affairs involving three phases of competition and repeated posing are excellent morale-builders, as well as good opportunities to critique progress and development. Bodybuilders can see if their assessment of themselves matches the assessment of their peers and the judges. Competitions can either be exhilarating or humbling.

For serious bodybuilders, the glitter of the contests eventually fades, and it's back to the weight room, to the relentless machines, to the strict diets, to the work, so they can be in even better shape–and maybe one day be the best in the world.

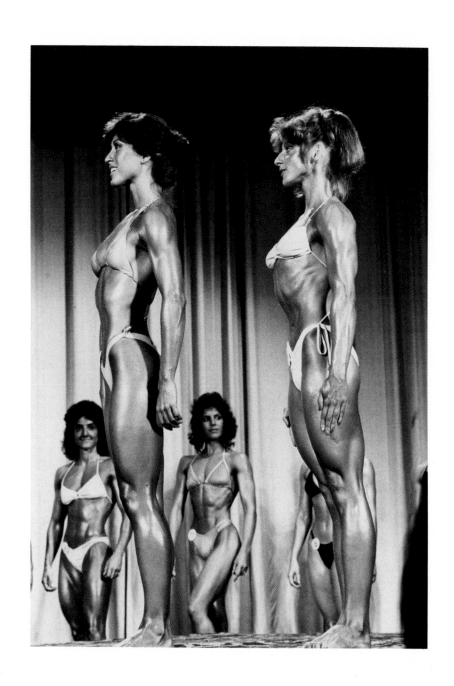

114

122

PART THREE

BEHIND

THE LENS ~

~THE PHOTOGRAPHERS

ROBERT MAPPLETHORPE

No photographer has made the impact of shooting a female bodybuilder that Robert Mapplethorpe has with his artistic interpretation of Lisa Lyon in the Viking Press book, *Lady*. Using Lyon as an art object photographed from all angles and in all kinds of settings, Mapplethorpe has created a new genre. His photographs of Lyon are currently on exhibit at the Leo Castelli Gallery in New York, the Rudigar Schottle Galerie in Munich, the Photografie Gallery in Dusseldorf and the Olympus Centre in London. Mapplethorpe has been both praised and criticized by New York critics—praised for his innovation and his technical expertise, and criticized for his tendency to shock his viewers. Innovative and sometimes startling, the dozen images of Lyon in this book are from the shooting for the book *Lady*. They constitute an entirely new direction in interpreting and portraying strong women.

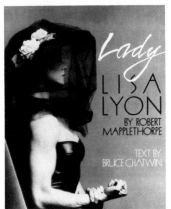

BILL HEIMANSON

In the late 1970s, women's bodybuilding came into its own, and Bill Heimanson, a Los Angeles photographer originally from Chicago, was on the scene to record the emergence of the sport. He began taking pictures at age 15 with a box camera, and he has been exploring the medium for more than 20 years. Heimanson has parlayed his interest in women's bodybuilding into several one-man shows. He is most skillful at capturing on film both the discipline and toughness of his subjects and their femininity. His favorite shot included here was taken in 1981 at the "Home of Champions" competition in Las Vegas. In this book, he is responsible for all of the photos of Michelle Howe and Reggie Bennett; pages 96, 97, 99 and 100 of the chapter on Michele Tierney; and pages 114, 116, 117 and 123 of the chapter on competition.

DAVID KEITH

David Keith pursued his education in photography at Tufts University in Medford, Massachusetts, at the University of California in Los Angeles, and finally at Art Center College of Design in Pasadena, California. During breaks in his college career, he worked at the *Amherst Record* in Massachusetts and on several independent photography projects. Upon graduation, he worked for two years as a lighting technician for *Sports Illustrated*. Keith is now the staff photographer for *Runner's World* and *Fit* magazines. His work in this volume marks his debut in bodybuilding photography. He is responsible for the chapters on Judy Hays-Ferguson and Patsy Chapman, and in the chapter on Michele Tierney, he is responsible for the photographs on pages 98, and 101 to 107. His favorite black-and-white photo depicts an elderly worker fashioning broom handles.

JOHN BALIK

"Bodybuilding has been a part of my life since my early teens," says John Balik. "I have participated in the sport as a competitor, official and as a contest promoter." As his interest in the sport grew, his scientific background (he has a degree in civil engineering) lured him into the study of nutrition. He eventually transformed his avocation into a mail-order vitamin company specializing in bodybuilding nutrition. Some five years ago, he became further involved when he decided to change his lifelong photographic hobby into a profession. Naturally, he specialized in bodybuilding. He currently writes about the sport, and has become well-known as one of the most technically excellent photographers of the sport. His favorite photograph is of Arnold Schwarzenegger checking a side chest pose at the original Gold's Gym in Venice in 1974, as Franco Columbu gazes in apparent disbelief. In this book, Balik's contributions are the chapters on Cheryl Howard and Chris Glass, as well as the competition photographs on pages 110 to 113 and 118 to 121.

JERRY FREDRICK

Jerry Fredrick has long been a photographer for *Sunset Magazine*, the magazine of the West. He has an alter-ego, however: Since 1979 he has been one of the premier bodybuilding photographers. In this book, he has contributed competition shots on the following pages: 115, 122, 124 and 125.